Romeo and Juliet

by William Shakespeare

Retold by Steve Barlow and Steve Skidmore

Illustrated by Mike Perkins

Series Editors: Steve Barlow and Steve Skidmore

Published by Heinemann Educational Publishers
Halley Court, Jordan Hill, Oxford OX2 8EJ
A division of Reed Educational and Professional Publishing Ltd

OXFORD   MELBOURNE   AUCKLAND
JOHANNESBURG   BLANTYRE   GABORONE
IBADAN   PORTSMOUTH NH (USA)   CHICAGO

First published 2000
2004   2003   2002   2001   2000
10   9   8   7   6   5   4   3   2   1
ISBN 0 435 21396 2

Illustrations by Mike Perkins
Cover design by Shireen Nathoo Design
Cover photo by Moviestore Collection
Designed by Artistix, Thame, Oxon
Printed and bound in Great Britain by Athenaeum Press Ltd

Tel: 01865 888058 www.heinemann.co.uk

Contents

Characters

The Capulet (Cap-you-let) Family

Lord Capulet –
Juliet's father

Juliet

Lady Capulet –
Juliet's mother

Tybalt (Tib-alt) – Juliet's cousin

Juliet's Nurse

The Montague (Mon-tag-you) Family

Lord Montague
– Romeo's father

Romeo

Benvolio (Ben-vo-leo) –
Romeo's friend

Others

**The Prince
of Verona**
(Vair-own-ah)

**Friar
Lawrence** –
a priest

Mercutio
(Mer-kew-she-
oh) – Romeo's
friend

Paris –
wants to
marry Juliet

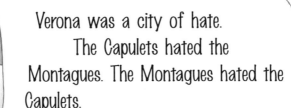

Verona was a city of hate.

The Capulets hated the Montagues. The Montagues hated the Capulets.

No one could remember why they had started to hate each other.

Over the years, there had been many fights between the two families.

It didn't take much to start a fight — just a word or even a look. Any reason was good enough.

Many people died in these fights. Hate leads to death.

But so can love...

CHAPTER 1

A fight

The sun beat down on Verona.

Two of Lord Capulet's servants were walking in the marketplace. Like the sun, their tempers were hot. They were looking for trouble. It didn't take them long to find it.

"Look over there," said one. He spat on the ground. "Montagues!"

Two of Lord Montague's men stood next to a fountain.

The Capulets walked over. The Montagues stood their ground.

As usual, a look led to an insult. Within the blink of an eye, four swords had been drawn.

"Stop! Put your swords away!"

All four servants turned towards the voice. It was Benvolio, a Montague.

At that moment Tybalt appeared. He was Lord Capulet's nephew.

"Help me to stop this fight, Tybalt," pleaded Benvolio.

Tybalt fingered his sword. He stared coldly at Benvolio.

"I hate all Montagues. And I hate you. Draw your sword!"

All hell broke out.

More and more men joined the fight. Montague fought Capulet. Capulet fought Montague. Capulet blood and Montague blood mixed on the ground.

Suddenly there was a sound of trumpets and a clatter of horses.

It was the Prince.

Everyone obeyed.

"Lord Capulet come here. You too, Lord Montague," ordered the Prince.

The two enemies moved forward.

The Prince's voice was hard. "The people of this city are tired of these fights. So am I! If your families break the peace again, you will pay for it with your lives!"

He looked around at the sorry scene. "Now go!"

CHAPTER 2

A party

Romeo was sitting on a wall. He looked miserable.

"What's the matter with him?" asked Mercutio. "Is he upset because he wasn't at the fight today?"

Benvolio laughed. "No. He's in love with Rosaline. But she isn't in love with him!"

Mercutio nodded. "He needs cheering up. I have the answer."

INVITATION
LORD AND LADY CAPULET invite you to a party to be held at their house, VERONA.

"I don't want to go," Romeo sighed. "And I'm sure that we won't be welcome at a Capulet party."

"That will make it more fun," said Mercutio. "We're going!"

The Capulets' party was in full swing when Romeo and his friends arrived.

Romeo was not enjoying the party. He was still feeling sorry for himself over Rosaline.

Then he saw a young girl he'd never seen before...

If there was ever such a thing as love at first sight, this was it!

Romeo had to speak to the girl. He began to push his way through the crowd of people. But he was being watched.

"It's Romeo! How dare he come here!" growled Tybalt. He turned to a servant. "Fetch me my sword!"

Lord Capulet heard Tybalt's shout. He hurried over. "What's the matter?" he asked.

"It's Romeo," Tybalt spat. "I'm going to teach him a lesson!" He grabbed his sword from the servant.

Lord Capulet held Tybalt's arm. "Leave him alone. I will not allow him to be harmed in my house."

"But, my Lord..."

"I said leave him alone!"

As Tybalt continued to argue with his uncle, Romeo reached the girl. He stood before her. She stared back at him.

It seemed that time had stopped. Music and guests melted into the background. They only had eyes for each other. And soon...

"Madam!" An old woman pulled the girl away from Romeo. "Your mother wants to see you."

"Yes, nurse." The girl turned back to Romeo and smiled. Then she disappeared into the crowd.

Romeo stood rooted to the spot. He had never met anyone so beautiful! Then a thought struck him. He didn't even know her name!

Suddenly someone grabbed hold of his arm. It was Mercutio.

"Quickly, we must leave." Mercutio nodded towards Tybalt and his friends. "They know who we are."

As Mercutio dragged him away, Romeo pointed towards the girl. "Do you know who she is?"

Mercutio looked up. "That's Juliet. She's Lord Capulet's daughter."

Romeo groaned. His new love was his old enemy!

Across the room, Juliet saw Romeo heading towards the door.

"Who is that?" she asked her Nurse.

"He's Romeo. He is the only son of Lord Montague."

A shudder went through Juliet's body.

CHAPTER 3

Love at first night

"Romeo! Romeo!" Benvolio shouted. There was no answer.

"Where's he got to?"

"Home to bed if he has any sense," replied Mercutio.

Romeo was hiding from his friends. He had decided not to go home. "How can I?" he whispered. "Juliet is here!"

Benvolio and Mercutio's shouts died down. Romeo was left on his own.

He began to climb a high wall. He reached the top and dropped into Capulet's garden.

Slowly, he made his way towards the house. He didn't want to get caught!

As he got closer to the house he saw a light shining from an upstairs window.

He looked towards the light. Someone was moving. It was Juliet!

She was standing on her balcony, gazing at the moon and stars. Romeo was dazzled by her beauty.

Romeo couldn't believe his ears!

"Then I will change my name!" he called out.

Juliet was startled. "Who's that?"

"I don't want to say my name," replied Romeo, "because you hate it."

"Is that Romeo?" she asked.

Romeo began to climb up to Juliet's balcony.

Juliet blushed. "Then you love me?" she asked.

"Yes."

"Lovers always say that." Juliet shook her head. "It's probably a lie."

"It's true!"

Juliet laughed at him. "Do you want me to say that I love you? That would be too easy! I should tell you to go away." She gave him a shy smile. "But you know that I love you. You heard me say it."

Juliet looked into Romeo's eyes. "Will you be my love? Will you marry me?"

"Is this just a dream?" thought Romeo. "Yes, I will," he replied.

Inside the house, an old woman's voice called out. "Juliet! Juliet!"

"It's my Nurse," whispered Juliet. "You must go."

CHAPTER 4

A wedding

The sun was beginning to rise as Friar Lawrence returned to his church. He had been collecting herbs and flowers. He used them to make medicines and potions.

"Friar Lawrence!"

The Friar turned round. He was surprised to see Romeo so early in the morning.

"Have you had any sleep?" he asked.

"No, Friar," replied Romeo. Then he told the Friar all about the Capulets' party and meeting Juliet.

"I thought you were in love with Rosaline," said Friar Lawrence.

"I have forgotten her. I love Juliet," replied Romeo.

The Friar shook his head. "Young people and love," he thought.

"We want to get married," said Romeo. "Will you marry us?"

And so the arrangements were made. Juliet sent her nurse to Romeo to find out where and when they would be married.

Romeo told none of his family or friends. Only Juliet's nurse and Friar Lawrence knew that Romeo and Juliet got married that afternoon.

CHAPTER 5

A death in the family

Benvolio and Mercutio sat in the hot afternoon sun.

"Let's go home, Mercutio," said Benvolio, "before we meet the Capulets. We don't want any trouble."

"Don't we?" Mercutio glared as Tybalt crossed the square.

I'm looking for Romeo. Have you seen him?

At that moment, Romeo appeared. He was returning home from his wedding.

Tybalt stood in front of him. "Romeo! You insulted me last night. Draw your sword!"

Romeo held his hands out. He couldn't fight Tybalt. Now he was married to Juliet, Tybalt was his cousin!

He shook his head and smiled. "But I love the name Capulet! As much as I love the name Montague. I will not fight you."

Mercutio was amazed. Romeo was refusing to fight!

"Put your swords away. The Prince told us not to fight!" Romeo tried to hold Mercutio back.

At that moment, Tybalt struck.

With those words, Mercutio died.

Romeo turned to face Tybalt.

"You have killed my friend," he cried.

Romeo drew his sword and killed Tybalt.

Benvolio grabbed Romeo by the arm. "You must get out of here! The Prince will have you killed if you stay in Verona."

Romeo dropped his sword. Weeping, he ran off.

CHAPTER 6

A farewell

At the Capulets' house, Juliet waited for Romeo. She had not heard about the fight.

Romeo had promised that they should run away together as soon as darkness fell. Juliet could hardly wait for the sun to go down.

There was a sound of footsteps on the stairs, and Juliet's door burst open. Her nurse rushed into the room. She was crying. "Oh God!" she wept. "Oh God have mercy on us all, he's dead!"

Juliet felt her blood run cold. "What do you mean? Is Romeo dead?" she whispered.

"Poor Tybalt!" sobbed the nurse.

Juliet shook her. "Who is dead? Romeo or Tybalt? Or both?"

"The Prince has sent Romeo away," sobbed the nurse. "He can't come back for you now. If the Prince finds him, he will kill him."

There was a noise from the balcony. Juliet spun round.

Romeo stood at the open window.

"You murderer!" Juliet flew at him in rage. A moment later, she flung her arms around him.

"You must be mad to come here. Where have you been?"

"With Friar Lawrence."

"You must go. The Prince is looking for you. You must get out of the city tonight!"

Romeo kissed her. He shook his head.

"Tomorrow."

The singing of birds woke Juliet. Romeo was standing by the window, looking out.

"Must you go?" sighed Juliet. "It's still dark."

Romeo turned to her. "It will be dawn soon."

"Don't go."

"All right." Romeo sat on the bed. "I'll wait here until the Prince's men come and find me, if that's what you want."

Juliet gasped in horror. "No, you must go now!" But as she pushed Romeo towards the window, her Nurse burst in at the door.

"Madam, your mother is coming!"

Romeo stepped onto the balcony. "Goodbye. One more kiss, then I'll go."

Romeo slipped into the shadows. Seconds later, Juliet's mother swept into the room.

"My dear girl," she cried, "I bring you good news!"

Juliet shook her head. "I can't think of any news that could make me happy today."

Lady Capulet took her hand. "You must stop weeping for Tybalt. Soon, you will be happy beyond your wildest dreams."

Juliet stared at her. "Why will I?"

"Because Paris has asked you to marry him!"

Paris? I can't marry Paris!

Lady Capulet gave her a cold stare. "Then tell your father so. Here he is."

Lord Capulet stood in the doorway, glaring. "What's this? You won't marry Paris?" The old man flew into a rage. "You brat!" He pointed at his daughter. "I have told Paris that you will marry him. If you don't, you can starve and die in the streets!"

Lord and Lady Capulet stormed out of the room. Juliet's nurse tried to comfort her.

"Don't cry!" she said. "Look at it this way. Romeo's gone. Forget him! Paris is a handsome man. He'll be a far better husband than Romeo!"

Juliet's heart sank. She knew that she could not trust her nurse anymore. "Go and tell my mother I am going to Friar Lawrence," she said. "I must ask God's forgiveness for making my father angry."

"That's a good girl." The nurse hurried away. Juliet was left on her own. She was in a terrible situation.

"Friar Lawrence will help me," thought Juliet.

CHAPTER 7

A deadly plan

Juliet hurried to see Friar Lawrence. But there was a shock in store for her. The friar was talking to Paris.

"Why is your wedding to Juliet going to take place so quickly?" asked Friar Lawrence.

"It was Lord Capulet's idea," said Paris, "It will help Juliet get over Tybalt's death." He turned and saw Juliet. "Good day, my lady." He smiled. "And my future wife."

Juliet looked at Friar Lawrence. "Shall I come back later?"

Paris raised a hand. "Don't let me keep you from your prayers." He kissed Juliet on her cheek, and left.

Juliet scrubbed angrily at her cheek.

"God help me!" she cried. "I have no hope!" She held out the knife she had brought from her room. "I would rather die than marry Paris."

Friar Lawrence took the knife from Juliet's hand.

43

"You must agree to marry Paris." Friar Lawrence continued. "Tonight, when you have gone to bed, drink this." He held up a small bottle. "It will send you into a sleep so deep that you will seem to be dead. Your skin will turn pale. Your body will turn cold. You will stop breathing."

Juliet gazed at him in horror.

"Your parents will weep. They will carry you to the Capulet tomb. But you will not be dead." The friar held out the bottle. "You will wake up in the tomb, forty-two hours after you have taken this potion."

Juliet took the bottle.

"I shall send a letter to Romeo," Friar Lawrence said. "I shall explain all this to him. He will come and take you from the tomb. Then you will be together."

That evening, Juliet kissed her mother 'goodnight'. She sent her nurse away.

"God knows when we shall meet again," she whispered.

She lay down on her bed. She took the top off the bottle. She was afraid.

"What if it doesn't work?" she thought.

She fetched the knife. "I shall keep it beside me," she thought. "A knife in the heart will always work."

She raised the bottle...

...and put it down again.

"Perhaps I shall wake up too early," she thought, "and be alone in a house of death. There might be no air. I might see ghosts, and go mad." She bit her lip. "It doesn't matter. I must do this for Romeo."

She raised the bottle to her lips...

...and drank.

Next morning, Juliet's nurse entered Juliet's room.

"Are you still in bed?" she said. "It's your wedding-morning. Get up you lazybones."

She threw open the curtains. Light poured into the room. The nurse turned towards the bed.

Her eyes widened.

Her screams woke everyone in the house.

CHAPTER 8

A problem

Friar Lawrence was feeling very pleased with himself.

Juliet's 'funeral' had taken place. She lay asleep in the Capulets' tomb, waiting for Romeo. Everything was going to plan.

Friar Lawrence looked up from his book as his friend Friar John came into the room. "Welcome back," he said. "Did you give Romeo my letter? How did he take the news?"

Friar John sat down. "I'm sorry, brother. I never reached Romeo."

Friar Lawrence felt an icy hand grab at his heart. "What do you mean?"

"I went to find another Friar to go with me. But he was visiting a sick family." Friar John rubbed his eyes. "The doctor came. He would not let us leave because we might spread the sickness."

"But the letter..." gasped Friar Lawrence.

"I could not take it. Here it is."

"So Romeo does not know it is a trick," said Friar Lawrence in a horrified voice. "He will think Juliet is dead." He closed his eyes in silent prayer. "My God! What will he do?"

A messenger from Verona found Romeo.

"My friend," Romeo said, "I am glad to see you! How is Juliet?"

The messenger looked worried. "She lies dead in the Capulet tomb," he said in a low voice. "Her soul is with the angels."

Romeo turned pale. "Then I have nothing to live for." He gave the messenger money from his purse. "Find horses for us both. I will go back to Verona tonight."

An hour later, Romeo was riding towards Verona with death in his heart. In his purse was a small bottle full of deadly poison.

"Well, Juliet," he said to himself, "I will be with you tonight!"

CHAPTER 9

A tragedy

The churchyard was dark, and still.

Paris stepped out of the shadows. He was crying. He began to lay flowers at the door of the Capulets' tomb. Then he heard a noise, and stepped back into the darkness.

Romeo moved silently between the graves to the Capulet tomb. He was with the messenger who had followed him to Verona.

Romeo turned to the messenger. "Go now," he said softly. "Whatever you see or hear, do not try to stop me. If you do, I shall tear you apart with my bare hands."

The messenger stepped back, trembling with fear.

But as Romeo turned towards the tomb, the messenger hid behind a gravestone. He wanted to see what would happen next.

Romeo took a crowbar from underneath his cloak. He forced it between the door and the wall of the tomb. He pulled with all his might. The lock snapped. The door to the tomb swung open.

A cold voice came from behind him.

"You are Romeo. You murdered Tybalt." It was Paris.

Romeo turned, slowly.

"Juliet died of a broken heart because you killed her cousin," said Paris. "Now I shall kill you."

Romeo's voice was harsh. "Leave me now, and I will let you live."

Paris drew his sword.

The fight was short. As Paris fell, the
messenger hurried away to tell the Prince
what he had seen.

Paris gripped Romeo's shoulder.

"I beg you," he whispered, "let me lie in the tomb with Juliet." Then he died.

Romeo stared at the pale, dead face.

"Paris!" Romeo sighed. "You wanted to marry Juliet. You shall be with her in death."

Romeo carried Paris into the tomb.

Then Romeo took Juliet's cold hand
between his own.

"You are still beautiful," he whispered,
"even in death."

Romeo took the bottle of poison from his purse and held it up.

"Now, Death, I am ready for you."

Romeo drank the poison, then for the last time, Romeo held Juliet in his arms.

Moments later, Friar Lawrence burst into the tomb. He saw the bodies of Paris and Romeo.

"Too late!" he moaned. "Too late!"

At the same moment, Juliet opened her eyes.

"Friar Lawrence!" She looked around at the dark walls of the tomb. "Where is Romeo?"

"Romeo is dead." He held out his hand to Juliet. "You must come with me. The Prince will be here soon."

Juliet looked down and saw the body of Romeo. She gave a moan and shook her head. "You go. I shall not leave my husband."

As Friar Lawrence ran away, Juliet knelt by Romeo. She took the poison bottle from his dead hand.

"Empty," she whispered.

From outside the tomb, she heard voices.

For the last time, she kissed Romeo.

She took the dagger from his belt.

CHAPTER 10

An ending

They all gathered in the tomb. The Prince. Friar Lawrence. Lord and Lady Capulet. Lord Montague.

Friar Lawrence told his story. All those who heard it wept.

Lord Montague wept. His wife had died that same night. Now his son was dead as well.

Lord and Lady Capulet wept. They had lost their daughter for a second time.

The Prince wept for his dead cousin, Paris.

"Lord Montague," he cried, "Lord Capulet! Do you see what has come of your quarrel?"

The Prince shook his head. "All are punished."

Lord Montague wiped tears from his face. "I shall have a golden statue made of Juliet."

"And I shall have a golden statue made

of Romeo," said Lord Capulet. He held out his hand.

Without a word, Lord Montague took it. Their long quarrel was over.

Author information

Romeo and Juliet was **William Shakespeare**'s first great success. His story of the "star-crossed lovers" is as popular today as it has ever been. The film by Baz Luhrmann starring Leonardo di Caprio was a worldwide hit.

Steve Barlow and Steve Skidmore say that *Romeo and Juliet* is one of their favourite Shakespeare plays. Their novel *Dream On* is based around a school production of *Romeo and Juliet*.

They have also adapted Shakespeare's *Twelfth Night* for **High Impact**.